T0072540

Restless Mind
and Other Poems

Ida Ngongkum

Langaa Research & Publishing CIG
Mankon, Bamenda

Publisher

Langaa RPCIG
Langaa Research & Publishing Common Initiative Group
P.O. Box 902 Mankon
Bamenda
North West Region
Cameroon
Langaagrp@gmail.com
www.langaa-rpcig.net

Distributed in and outside N. America by African Books Collective
orders@africanbookscollective.com
www.africanbookscollective.com

ISBN-10: 9956-552-97-6

ISBN-13: 978-9956-552-97-9

© Ida Ngongkum 2021

Table of Contents

Foreword

William Wordsworth wrote of poetry as "a spontaneous overflow of powerful feelings" arising from "emotions recollected in tranquillity". To complement Wordsworth's often quoted statement; Robert Graves writes that to be a poet "is a condition, not a profession". Hence, it is the human condition that inspires poetry. Poetry therefore, is the rhythm of the human mind decoded from the heartbeat of everyday life.

Each writer is a reflection of his/her time and that time counts in evaluating the history of literary traditions whether it was the best of the writings or not. Ida Ngongkum is a young Cameroonian poet who, like other writers, works on the basis of her time, a fact which inspires Philip Levine to caution: "Listen to these young poets and you will discover the voice of the present and hear the voice of the future…."

She belongs to a literary tradition sustained by the younger generation of writers who imitate the elders but can also do more than those who have gone before them. As a young poet, Ida draws inspiration from a parentage imbued with the literary arts, her father being an all-pervading playwright and poet, her mother a proficient fiction writer, she combines parental influence and recollections of her times to forge her own niche.

In her collection of poems, *Restless Mind*, the young poet turns herself inside out to enrich our understanding of the human condition, the emotion, the grief, passion, the love, and everything that is human that she has experienced in her youth. Many of the poems are concerned about humanity which is always berserk with issues as reflected in the title of the collection "Restless Mind". The poems show the poet's concerns about the world at the centre of which is the effort to survive in an alien world. The mind, of course, cannot be calm in a tumultuous universe, a universe so well described in the poems as "crazed hullabaloo", a world where God is forsaken and a world in which peace is hard to find.

Like every good poet, she instils hope in humankind through visionary hints. The solution to pain and sorrow is to embrace the life beyond. She adopts an advisory tone that spells out the idea of having a purpose in life without which life is a failure and causes overwhelming sorrows. As in "Lessons", poetry becomes indeed a tool for teaching and learning lessons from life experiences: "you have taught me to laugh to smile through pain". Poetry teaches how a poet should feel, love, and seek truth in trying to understand and experience the world around her and engage the world of art.

Although some poets convey their message obliquely, Ida Ngongkum opens up her emotional life for all to see, feel and learn from it.

The style is simple but the message is profound. The reader will find in the collection fascinating poems that will inspire readers of all ages.

John Nkemngong Nkengasong
Writer and Critic

I

I WRITE

The words at the tip of my tongue,
Are eager to find their way out.
Though my emotions are in bitter turmoil within
And I am possessed by a rage that caters not for any whim,
I try my best to sit still, to keep calm and to shut up.
Then I write.

I write of my woes,
Each stroke of my pen echoes the throng of my voice.
I write of my fears,
The ink of my pen displays the darkest of them all.
I write of my tears,
Of hurt and scars borne over the years.
I write of One that seeks to consume me,
One who absolutely terrifies me.
I write of my cries,
A river of sorrows that threatens to overwhelm me.

I do not write because I'm scared to express
What I really feel inside.
I rather fear that my stunted speech
Will not be adequate enough to convey
How I really feel inside.
So I write.
I write of a song,

Which has never been sung.
I write of words,
Which have never been spoken.
I write of a tale,
Which may never unfold.

And though it threatens
To eat me up from deep within,
I sit still, keep calm, shut up
And I write.

II

WORDS

Words.
They speak to each man in a unique way.
Words.
You never know what they'll do
'Til they're spoken to you.

III

VOICE IN MY HEAD

The Voice in my head
Has a mind of Her own.
Louder than my own voice,
Yet serene in all Her poise.
She says not what I say
She's all craftiness and mischief.
Discretely, Her seeds are sown.
In my ignorance, are they watered to bloom.

IV

FIDUS ACHATES

'Twas said by our fathers afore,
A faithful friend, who can find?
Words but galore
It originates from the mind.

Fidus Achates, faithful friend
None but thee can me comprehend!
'Midst the tears, the hurt, the pain
Thou bidd'st me rise, stay true to my name.
"Gallant warrior, fortunate at that
Never relent, live up to the task!
Cling to thy God, though many a dart
When all is o'er, in His Glory shalt thou bask."

Thou hast been there, my counselor friend
Fashioned together from time beyond sphere.
Fidus Achates, faithful friend,
Before thee, unto thee, my heart will I bare.

V

EACH MAN HIS METRE

'Dig deeper', they say
'Look within and find yourself'.
'Persevere', they say
'What doesn't kill makes strong'.

What if finding myself were not from within?
What if strength were not to define me?
What if I were made of something different,
Different from what the world perceives to be norm?
What if they are different methods, but the same values?
What if?
What doesn't kill, does make strong.
It doesn't say exactly what it is that kills.
What doesn't kill me, may kill you:
For "A man's food is another's poison."

It is not my place or yours
To tell another what they can or cannot do.
Nor is it our place to judge them
Based on what they can or cannot do.

Let each man be his own metre.

VI

RESTLESS MIND

Wandering heart, restless mind
Wondering mind, do you mind?
I need my peace! I need my quiet!
I need some time alone, some time in my closet!
You do not listen, restless mind
And keep creeping up on me,
Smothering my calmness.
How am I to think, restless mind?
I am expected to be rational, for crying out loud!
I need my wits settled all about me
Not jumbled up in some crazed hullaballoo.
You will do well to be calm, restless mind
I really mind, that you, restless mind, do not mind!

VII

MUSING

The preoccupations of a troubled mind are but many…

Wounds bleeding anew
Past scars once more torn apart.
They keep me wondering, keep me pondering
Lost in a vortex of tumultuous thoughts
Burdened by infernal struggles
Blinded by greed and deceit
Entangled in an intricately spun web of sorrows
I am so caught up in my own world
That I can hardly hear the call to Help nearby.

As many as the stars in a cloudless sky…

Have I no issue?
Will the torment ever end?
Am I so deaf, that I do not hear this Call to Help
Or without sight, that I do not see this Light at the tunnel's
end?
No! It cannot be so!
For I shall certainly break free!
But again, at what cost? Am I willing to pay the price?
Yet, I yearn for freedom, I yearn for this Light.
Am I willing to let go of this thing that causes me pain?

VIII

LIFE BEYOND

There is love beyond colour,
Life beyond race.
A sweetness to trivial things
Time can't erase.
Quit mulling and worrying
Over things you can't change,
There's life beyond sorrow, heart ache and pain.

There is life beyond deception,
You should know by now!
Friend, foe or family,
Will someday let you down!
Quit depending and expecting
Please, start self-constructing,
For there's life beyond people, position and power!

There is life beyond wealth,
Ethnicity and tribe.
Life beyond intellectualism,
Life beyond the bar!
There's life beyond the weekend,
I'd rather you see this now-
That there's life and much more, to everything around.

IX

MONSTER WITHIN

Splaying fingers upon the lustrous chest
Contemplating its magnificence
Sparkling with every light, robed in diamonds
Catching the eye of every passerby.

Musing as to what lay beneath
Lifting but not opening
Opening but not thinking
Thinking but not seeing
Seeing but not speaking
Speaking but not listening
Listening but not hearing
Hearing but not understanding
Understanding but not comprehending
Such is the mystery of the monster within.

Darkness to every soul
Gloom behind every smile
Malice following every good
The monster- Subterfuge.
Pretty on the outside, hollow within
Cramped with all sorts of villainy
Hate to every love
Tear behind every laughter
War following every peace
Such is the nature of the monster within.

Now,
Closing without shutting
Shutting without locking
Locking without sealing
Sealing…but I'm fastening!

X

DARK PLACE

I am in a dark place,
I know neither friend nor foe.
A dangerous place, this dark place
For I know not where to go.

I am in a dark place,
Far off from Ones adored.
Pitch black, this dark place
Battlefield of mind and word.

XI

STRESSED

I'm at my wits' end, I'm stressed!
Recently I figured out that
It is a thing to be alive, quite another to be living
And the latter, has me stressed!

'Why?' Many ask,
For I am un-accomplished in years (to them)
And have experienced not many a thing.
My response:
'Life is a progression of uncertainty,
An enormous game of probability.
This alone suffices to scare me,
And that is why I'm stressed!'

'It is limit upon deadline,
Task upon errand,
An endless cycle, living!
Left to right, Up and down
Not a moment's rest,
How would I not be stressed?'

XII

THEM

"Away! Away!" I heard a shout.
"Keep all mares at bay! Hal's got a bout."
Standing perplexed at the mutinous cries,
I had eyes for nothing, other than them.

Hal, a magnificent beast was he
At the acme of his life, an abysmal point was it
Sire to thousands of geldings,
His complacence was not understood by them.

Toiled and toiled throughout the day,
Adumbrate, yes, this I may
Hal at the Cairn, I cannot but say,
I bet you are as confused as them.

Reclining upon the mound known by most as the Cairn,
He bellowed a neigh, propounding his End.
Woeful, piteous and subdued a sound,
Perceived by all, imbibed by them.

XIII

HYPOCRITES

They act like we chose our names
Like we grew our own face,
Like we had a say in our race…

They pretend they care
Truth is, they've eyes solely for our flair,
So they lure us into their Lair.

XIV

ALONE

Alone…
The words echo in my mind, their brand fresh upon my
heart.
Alone…
Beloveds taken from you, untimely, or so you say.
Alone…
You see so many, you are surrounded by so many
All smiles and happy faces, but fundamentally, you are
Alone…
'Tis but a basic truth each man needs to understand;
For whether ye have family, friends, foe or nought,
In the end, we are all
Alone.

XV

POISON

Poison.
She seeped through the pores
Infusing its weary hollows.

Poison.
Paving her way slowly to *M'akoma*[1],
Corrupting fiber and entity
Of this defenseless being.

Poison,
She's a deadly snare.
Once she's got you, my friend,
You're better off if you never were!
She makes, breaks, un-makes and un-breaks.

Poison,
You see, my friend,
Had M'akoma obliviously dancing to her band.
In less than no time,
He was eating out of her hand.

Flee, my friend, from Poison
Vain, vile and fickle is she truly
Yet, masquerades as everything holy.

---

[1] *"M'akoma" is an Akan word which means "My heart".*

17

XVI

WHEN I'M ABOUT TO SURRENDER

As the dawn of light breaks yonder,
Shadows of darkness are cast asunder
Mother, she emerges like thunder.
Before the sun is overhead
The gifts of nature doth she plunder.
Many like me do ponder;
Surreal caliber of woman, what a wonder!

My father, nature's banker,
Transforms life's every gallop into a canter!
To children, he may be Santa
To me, my life–defending panther.
My heart leaps without bound, without border,
Whenever I sit to remember
It is he who stirs me up when I'm about to surrender.

Together, we are stronger.
We work faster, we walk further
We rely on one another.
Formidable support system, no one works harder!
My heart leaps without bound, without border,
Whenever I sit to remember,
That family indeed, lasts forever!

They never falter,
Hardly do they blunder

They make me grow fonder
'Cause day by day, their intrinsic facets I discover.
My heart leaps without bound, without border,
Whenever I sit to remember
It is they who spur me up when I'm about to surrender.

XVII

PURPOSE

Had fear a name,
It would be called failure!
In all its menacing allure
Its only aim, to maim.

Shrouded in fear,
Is the man without purpose.
Overwhelmed by fallacious sorrows
Too great for his fickle heart to bear.

I fear for a tragic end,
Should he his issues not resolve.
Like the sugar that refuses to dissolve,
Shall his turmoil last, world without end.

XVIII

THE FOLLY OF MY WOMAN

It was in the rainy season that I married her
Wild and untamed, a thing of beauty
Jewel of my heart, brimming with potential and resources
She was indeed a sight to behold
This wife of my captivity.

In the cold of our incarceration
We huddled together to comfort each other.
Her face mirrored my gauntness
My plight reflected in her eyes
The chains brought us closer in sweat, blood and tears.

And then one day, our liberation came!
We were once again free to make our own choices
I chose to stick with her, she chose to stay with me
And so was our union forged
Within the walls of the Evil Circus.

My woman was content in our early years
Our pledge, one of mutual understanding and growth
And grow did we as the years went by.
Yet we were still marionettes
Under the Evil Puppet Master's control.

She rebelled in our jubilee
More than fifty years into our union!

She says she has been repressed, cornered into silence,
Marginalized and abused of her rights
This is the folly of my woman.

She demands that we part ways
But I am rather unyielding
She is enraged, fuming and on a destructive spree
All in a bid to be rid of me.
Is this quite a folly? Or is my woman right?

XIX

CHILD OF PROMISE

A tale foretold of the birth of a bairn,
As fair as day and calm as night.
Spun from truth, partly myth
Among siblings, was she fifth.

Truth be told, we did not know
What the future held for this bairn below.
Ordinarily uncommonly favored,
She paved her way through life, this dungeon.
Grace did unwind the shackles that did her bind,
For she was daughter to Grace and Favor-
Child of Promise.

XX

PREJUDICE

For once, she wished they'd see
Beyond the permanent lines marring her forehead,
Beyond the stoic countenance she always bore
Beyond the ragged clothes on her back
And the shoes that adorned her feet.
Beyond her curves or the lack thereof,
Beyond the colour of her skin
And the texture of her hair,
Beyond the slant of her eyes and the lisp of her tongue,
She wished they'd see beyond their Prejudice.

She hoped they'd see
That she too deserved a Voice
And she deserved their acceptance.
She hoped they'd see
That she was able and capable
As much as anyone of them was.
She hoped they'd see
That she too deserved second chances,
That she was as human as they were, and above it all
She hoped they'd see beyond their Prejudice.

XXI

LOST LOVE

Piece by piece, I come apart
In sorrow and anguish my heart is rent.
Understand me, this I pray,
Amidst this epiphany of turmoil and misconception-
For I am the very knife that butchers my torn heart.

Mayhap I never understood the meaning of Love
But you were my first, You my best friend.
From lives shared to tears spent and lessons learned
You had been there for me,
I never was good enough for you.
Mind-withering agony is what I feel
As I sit in my corner while you are in yours.
Strangely friends, Friendly strangers
Toasting to this really sad, sad song.
I'm a bag of convoluted troubles, I must say
But never did I anticipate we were going to end this way.

Two years of a decade short,
Still yet, I mourn the love of a friend lost...
The years go by, and I come to understand
Though we've grown together, we've come apart.
Undoubtedly and forever, you remain in my heart.

XXII

SHADOW

She was, once again, but a shadow of her former self;
Hollow, decrepit and empty within.
The days of happiness had been fulfilling, albeit short.
It had seemed all too good to be true-
The blissful chatter, the peace, the contentment
The acceptance, the compassion and kindness,
All had been a front.
And it had been savagely torn away.
In its stead was left a Void,
One she suspected no one could fill.
Afterall, she had tried it all –
The drinks, the drugs, the coke
She had pushed herself out of her comfort zone
All in a bid to find acceptance.
And oh did she find it!
Or at least she thought she did,
For no sooner than she had 'found it'
Had it been ferociously ripped away.
Grief, despair and self loathing were all that remained.

XXIII

YEARNING

The one you'd run to
before every verse…
The one you'd come to
Whether filled or in thirst…
Every frown, Smile or Tear,
Every struggle…tiny or too great to bear
Whether you're down or at your very best,
I want to be the First.

XXIV

KALEIDOSCOPE

We could see it in his eyes
The passion and fury, intertwined
Like the altering motifs of The Kaleidoscope
So was he, unstable, changing, vascillating.
We heard it also in his cries
The dementia and acumen, intervolved…
Yet, *"un-existent remains art*
Which decrypts from his face,
The constitution of man's mind" -
The Kaleidoscope.

XXV

THE DREAM

I dreamed a dream of the man with a thousand names
A dream of a thousand laughs,
A dream of a thousand heartbreaks.
Alter ego is he, the man of my dream
Friend, critic and confidant, molded into one.
Fated against all odds,
We shunned the scorns of men.
We lived, we laughed, we loved
We warred, we teared, we fought.
And so real was each one,
I felt my gut clench as my pillow drenched
I felt my heart leap, each thump out of beat.
On an anguished note, did this unveiling end
That the man of my dream left,
As I awoke from my dream of a thousand heartbreaks
A dream of a thousand laughs,
A dream of the man with a thousand names.

XXVI

UNVEILING

Flawed, Imperfect, Incomplete
The sight of the one who sees but does not See.
Understanding, is Seeing
The ephemerality of a thing.
Yet, it's picture-perfect to me
Flaws, thorns, all as meant to be
Concealed beneath the scales, can't you See?
More than picturesque, it's Perfect,
To me!

XXVII

FRAGMENTS

Bitter, broken and battered
Is the heart I present you.
By my own hand crushed beyond repair,
And utterly humiliated.
These fragments aren't of worth to you;
For you see through my façade,
You see beyond this mirage of tumultuous feelings,
You hear the whimpering, mourning and weeping.
I rend my garments, with hope that I'll be forgiven
With hope that I can successfully piece together,
Fragments of a heart that's been torn asunder.
Then will I present to you
Some semblance of a heart that's whole
One that desires to be fully yours.
'Nay, child', you say
'Bring the pieces; come just as you are--
Bruised, lost and empty.
These fascinating Fragments, they are your life
And each one beautifully tells a story...
I'm interested in the fragments of your life
For in the mosaic they create lies your glory.'

XXVIII

LESSONS

On my own, have I learnt to live;
To fuel the tank of determination,
To fan the flames of desire,
To let ambition burn brightly.

You have taught me to laugh;
To smile through the pain,
To be cheerful in face of oppression,
To be glad, amidst opposition.

I am learning to love;
To give a little more freely,
To sacrifice in earnest,
To look beyond the pain, to forgive.

XXIX

RESCUE

The word strikes a chord in my innermost being.
Rescue.
For as long as I can remember,
I had been drinking from the deep well of Sorrows.
Rescue.
Atop his valiant steed to break the invisible bonds
Bonds of the silent suffering I'd borne throughout the years.

XXX

THE WORLD AWAITS

I feel Him in the breeze
I see Him all around me.
That still small Voice says:
"The world awaits you."

And Yes!
The world awaits me!
Not as a thing of beauty or frailty,
But a figure of power and authority.

The world awaits me...

XXXI

FOOL FOR RIGHT

You have worn your 'youth' well
And it looks exceptionally good on you.
Because you have refused to see this evil I see,
Your estranged mind has made for herself a barricade.
You would rather honey-coated poison
As opposed to flint-cutting verity.
Your presumed Euphoria is but a fleeting emotion,
Deceiving you into believing that she would halt
The bitterness of what is and is to come.

Your Conscience cannot be at peace
You have betrayed her, you have betrayed me.
It saddens my heart that you indulge in immorality
The lust of the flesh, of the eye and the pride of life
These have become the bread for your soul.
What happened to our dreams of creating a better world?
What happened to our visions of integrity and moral
rectitude?
You astound me friend, you really do
You sold your 'Right' at the cost of your Light.

What else do you want from me?
You who once said I was too young to perceive,
You now call me old-fashioned, a dimwit and nitwit
Simply because I have refused to succumb
To this treacherous way of life?

I can't deny it, blackness gnaws at every man's heart
But here, my friend, lies the difference between you and me-
I would rather be a fool for Right
Than with my own hand snuff out my Light.

I am extremely proud of how well I've aged
The seasons have hardened me
And I have seen beyond my years.
I can no longer hold the gastritis of my silence
For this darkness which has you in her claws
Is the cankerworm plaguing our society.
Should we not rise against her now
We would be forever engulfed in misery…
Guard your Light, and let it Shine!

XXXII

REDEFINED

Your love has redefined Me
For you see beyond my shame
Through to the beauty in my scars.

The troubles, the trials, have redefined Us
They have made us much stronger
And indeed, better together.

Together, we will redefine You
Your perspective and outlook
On life, a much higher calling.

XXXIII

THE PATH

So long, so often have we trod
The ancient path of life
Sometimes boisterous, sometimes not
Seeded with envy and strife.
Looking back with a nod
At the times we fought to survive
When for our own backs we made a rod
Yet we thank Him we're alive!

Looking back at our egocentricity
The world revolving around us, we felt a must
Forgetting our posterity,
That one day we all return to dust.
It never will be a matter of prosperity
Prosperity fades in a gust.
There was and always will be disparity
Between the unrighteous and the just.

Proud, arrogant and disdainful
None else but we
Yet so very painful
As the tale turns out to be
He who is so Faithful
Whose eyes our every deeds did see
Made our subjects joyful
Answering their every plea.

In no time, we became nothing
Wealth was turned to ash.
He who knows everything
Our egos did dash.
With time we learnt something
Which no remorse can patch-
That human life means everything
To Him who made all from scratch.

Predators became prey
Kings became slaves
No one was held at bay
None, not even the Braves.
The path, the vicious cycle
Engulfed our every cries
Hopeless, but for a Miracle
Our intended haven- insatiable fires.

Yea, the Truth in the lines past
Redeemed us from our doom
We learned and did hold fast
To the promise of ending gloom.
Our next stop along this path
Will be to spread the news:
"Tenacity incurs Wrath,
From heathen and self-professed Jews."

To this life, there is life
To this life, there is death
Would you rather the knife
Or rest upon your Saviour's hearth?

XXXIV

ENIGMA

As I watched, I saw the years go by.
"Oh!" I wondered, "How futile is life!"
'Tis nothing but a sporadic puzzle
Left uncovered to many, yet to be discovered.
Then said I to myself
"There is something I must assimilate;
Why do the wicked live, while the righteous perish?
The unjust survive, while the just, life doth punish?"

Though I donned the wisdom of men,
I gained naught but confusion without end.
Then I sought to question He
Who didst make you and me
For this is something un-understood
By plenty (there are many in my hood)
What happened to the adage that says
"Hard work surely pays?"

No matter how far I went
Or how deep I swam
Or how high I flew
My questions to this day
Are without answer.
It's comforting to know, however,
That many like me
Are unable to decipher this enigma.

Oh! The answer from the Mighty One
Was as simple as this:
"Child, hold fast to what you know
To what you have seen and what you have learnt
The virtues now may seem without reward
But remember, I have the final Word!"
Tarry as it may, do not your vision dis-concentrate
The End bears all answers to this mystery, puzzle, enigma.

XXXV

REDEMPTION

Turns upon me a shadow
The darkness of night closing in.
Thinking, brows creased in a furrow
Voices in my head unending, a tremendous din.

Yes, it's all coming back
In bits, in flashes, in bursts
My past beckons like an enchanting lark
Moments, when prized possessions were my lusts.

My captors are at my heels
Seemingly a journey of no return
They demand I pay the bills
Else forever with them burn.

It's a war within my soul
Taking over my entirety
One that I just can't control
In all its ferocity.

My Knight-in-shining-armour
Appears upon the scene
He puts an end to this clamour
And to this titanic din.
I gaze upon Him, amid sob and confusion
His scars payment for my tribulation,
His loving me without condition
O Yes, Perfect Redemption!

Printed in the United States
by Baker & Taylor Publisher Services